A Working Marriage

On the Same Team

A Working Marriage

A Working Marriage

On the Same Team

A Working Marriage

ONEDIA NICOLE GAGE, PH. D., CLC

A Working Marriage

Dedication

For the couples who just needs a bit of encouragement

For the couples who are sleeping in separate rooms

For the couples who are sleeping with other people

For the couples who are in mediation

For the couples who just filed divorce papers

This is for you.

Because you are holding this book, then your marriage is not over.

Library of Congress

On the Same Time

A Working Marriage

All Rights Reserved © 2025

Onedia N. Gage, Ph. D., CLC

No part of this book may be reproduced or transmitted in
Any form or by any means, graphic, electronic, or mechanical,
Including photocopying, recording, taping, or by any
Information storage or retrieval system, without the
Permission in writing from the publisher.

Purple Ink, Inc. Press

For Information address:
Purple Ink, Inc.
1202 E. 1st St., 14931,
Humble, TX 77347
www.purpleink.net ♦ onediagage@purpleink.net

Onedia Gage Speaks

www.onediagagespeaks.com ♦
onediagage@onediagagespeaks.com

ISBN:

978-1-939119-83-4

Printed in the United States

SCRIPTURES

Leave and cleave.

Genesis 2:24

He that finds a wife, finds a good thing.

Proverbs 18:22

What God has joined, let no man put asunder.

Matthew 19:6

Love extravagantly.

1 Corinthians 13:13b MSG

Love.

Ephesians 3:14-21

A Working Marriage

Other Books by Onedia N. Gage, Ph. D., CLC

Are You Ready for 9th Grade . . . Again? A Family's Guide to Success
As We Grow Together Daily Devotional for Expectant Couples
As We Grow Together Prayer Journal for Expectant Couples
As We Grow Together Bible Study: Her Workbook
As We Grow Together Bible Study: His Workbook
Because I Do: A Working Marriage—Her Workbook
Because I Do: A Working Marriage—His Workbook
The Best 40 Days of My Life: A Journey of Spiritual Renewal
The Blue Print: Poetry for the Soul
From Fat to Fit in 90 Days: A Fitness Journal
From Two to One: The Notebook for the Christian Couple
Hannah's Voice: Powerful Lessons in Prayer
The Heart of a Woman: The Depth of Her Soul
Her Story The Legacy of Her Fight: The Bible Study
Her Story The Legacy of Her Fight: The Devotional
Her Story The Legacy of Her Fight: The Legacy Journal
Her Story The Legacy of Her Fight: Prayers and Journal
I Am.: 90 Days of Powerful Words: Affirmation and Advice for Girls
ily! A Mother-Daughter Relationship Workbook
In 90 Days: What Will You Do?
In Her Own Words: Notebook for the Christian Woman
In Purple Ink: Poetry for the Spirit
In Your Hands: A Dad's Impact on His Daughter's Self-Esteem
Intensive Couples Retreat: Her Workbook
Intensive Couples Retreat: His Workbook
Living A Whole Life: Sermons Which Prompt, Provoke, and Provide Life
Living An Authentic Life
Love Letters to God from a Teenage Girl
The Measure of a Woman: The Details of Her Soul
The Notebook: For Me, About Me, By Me
The Notebook for the Christian Teen
On the Same Team
On This Journey Daily Devotional for Young People
On This Journey Prayer Journal for Young People
On This Journey Prayer Journal for Young People, Vol. 2
One Day More Than We Deserve Prayer Journal for the Growing Christian

A Working Marriage

Promises, Promises: A Christian Novel
Queen in the Making: 30-Week Bible Study for Teen Girls
Queen in the Making: 30 Week Bible Study for Teen Girls Leader's Guide
The Secrets of My Success: Business Coaching How does she do it? Who does she think she is?
Serve the Staff: The Impact of a Healthy Social-Emotional Climate and Culture
She Spoke Volumes... And Then Some
Six Months of Solitude: The Sanctity of Singleness Notebook
Six Months of Solitude: The Sanctity of Singleness Prayers and Journal
There's a Queen Within: Her Journey to Building Self—Worth
Tools for These Times: Timely Sermons for Uncertain Times
The Vision Notebook
Walking Tall with a Broken Life
What Did You Say?: Affirmations. Encouragement. Motivation.
With a Crown and No Home: Spiritual Messages for Women
With An Anointed Voice: The Power of Prayer
A Woman Like Me: A Bible Study for Women to Survive Our Times
A Woman Like Me: A Daily Devotional for Women to Survive Our Times
A Woman Like Me A Sermonic Study: Lessons for Us Women to Survive Our Times
Yielded and Submitted: A Woman's Journey for a Life Dedicated to God
Yielded and Submitted: A Woman's Journey for a Life Dedicated to God An Intimate Study
Yielded and Submitted: A Woman's Journey for a Life Dedicated to God Prayers and Journal

The Nehemiah Character Series

Nehemiah and His Basketball
Nehemiah and His Big Sister
Nehemiah and His Bike
Nehemiah and His Flag Football Team
Nehemiah and His Football
Nehemiah and His Golf Clubs
Nehemiah and Math
Nehemiah and the Bully

ON THE SAME TEAM

Nehemiah and the Busy Day
Nehemiah and the Class Field Trip
Nehemiah and the Substitute for the Substitute
Nehemiah Can Swim
Nehemiah Found the Mud
Nehemiah Reads to Mommy
Nehemiah Writes Just Like Mommy
Nehemiah, the Hot Dog, and the Broccoli
Nehemiah's Family Vacation
Nehemiah's Favorite Teacher Returns to School
Nehemiah's First Day of School
Nehemiah's Sister Moved
Nehemiah's Visit to the Hospital

A Working Marriage

Dear God,

I know that I am in Your handbook of grace. I never wanted to be divorced and always wanted to be married, even though how much work it may be.

I watched my grandparents take of their spouses and all of that demonstrated love to me. This is the epitome of love. For that reason, I thank You for helping me to get this project done.

Thank You for letting me see the On the Same Team in action with a couple that still take my breath away, even though they have been deceased many years.

When the epiphany overcame me, I shuttered! How do You allow a four-year-old flag football quarterback teach me about marriage on the football? I am grateful that I caught on so that I would be able to share Your gift with others.

When I get the chance again, I will not squander it or take it for granted. I realize that everyone is not trained to be a successful couple. I realize that I need to exercise my understanding about the nuances of marriage and what causes the relationship to deplete.

In all my ways I will acknowledge You and I pray that You direct my path. When he finds me, I hope that I will know and I will acquiesce, becoming his bride and having the best zeal, better than those who I mistakenly offered my zeal to.

I love You. I thank You for loving me. I thank You for making me lovable and tenacious, intoxicating and overwhelming, outrageous and outlandish.

Sincerely,

A Working Marriage

Onedia

The Future Bride/Wife/Teammate/Wearing Matching Jerseys

ON THE SAME TEAM

DEAR COUPLE,

Many of us grew up with dysfunctional or absent marriages. Statistically speaking you are not supposed to be married. You are not even supposed to want to be married. You were not even supposed to get married. And you are certainly not supposed to be in this room trying to have a better marriage. When you told people where you were going, they are still laughing at you. Followed up with "that workshop will never work. Marriages do not get better at workshops." But here you are. Whether you came because she threatened you or he has already moved out, you have decided to fight for a future that you have never seen an example of. Likewise, you are trying to leave a legacy that you can give to your children that they can use and be proud of. Being here takes courage, in front of all these people who have similar issues as you: their marriage is likewise broken and in need of encouragement. The more important similarity is that you are here, you have decided that the time you spend here is worth it to enhance your marriage, and you are invested at a high level. Your presence says that your marriage matters to you!

When you consider the word legacy, it is defined as anything handed down from the past. Sometimes legacy is associated with money. How many of us will inherit anything other than debt? Not many but we have all inherited some family and its issues and activities. All of which add up to the legacy you have. Some of us have never seen a successful marriage. Others of us have never seen a healthy marriage. Still others of us have never even seen a marriage in our families. Needless to say, we are up against incredible odds!

So based on the legacy we have, we should not even know what marriage is. We are not destined to have a great marriage. But you have taken it upon yourself to challenge that legacy, your personal lineage, to change the course of that legacy spoke unto us, just by you being here. The fact that you showed up is enough notification that you are considering a different present and legacy.

The legacy we create involves an element of change that requires work. Marriage is hard work! Make no mistake! It is daily work! No breaks! No brakes! No vacations! No time-outs! The first step to establishing the legacy you desire is to remember what your spouse needs from you, expects from you, and gives to you through their lives, their heart, their sacrifices, their energy, their time, and their talent. Your spouse does things that they have never done as a spouse and they give more of themselves than they ever had. Do not take your spouse for granted. Emotional neglect happens in marriages daily because we assume that our spouse is okay with everything we are doing. Give your spouse what they ask and ultimately require of you. Giving your mate what they need will allow for your marriage to be better and more engaging.

Your marriage deserves the best of you, your time, your energy, and your focus. How do I do that? You have to keep your marriage first—this means that you protect the time for your marriage. Give it ALL of you! It deserves all of you. Your marriage has to last for the rest of your life, so you need to do what is necessary to ensure that your spouse knows that she/he is first right after God. Your time is valuable to your mate. Do you remember when you were in love with your mate? You could not wait until you were in her presence again. Your workday was too long. Traffic was too much. All you wanted to do was to see your mate. Now that you are married, but you are not in a hurry to get home. You are not thinking of her as much. Your dialogue and communication are severely lower, strained and critically different.

ON THE SAME TEAM

She notices. She questions you. You deny. She argues her point with irrefutable evidence. You continue the denial response. You are successful. She is right. She is hurt. She goes into your bedroom and cries herself to sleep. You sleep with the remote. Your marriage just changed.

Your time and dedicated conversation are needed in order for your marriage to thrive. Decide to breathe life into your marriage with words, deeds, time, energy, and attentiveness.

Another point on the best of you. Her and his homes need to be the picture of excellence. You need to bring your talents, skills and resources home. There are husbands who construct beautiful homes or theatre homes or gardens, but they never complete their homes or its projects. She is a master chef but he eats his meals out of a box or bag.

This is not giving the best of yourself to your mate.

A man I counseled shared that his wife would not have sex with him. I asked him why not. He said that she was tired. I then had him to describe her day as best he could. She was an elementary school teacher. They have three boys, ages 3, 5, and 7. She leaves work a four o'clock. She picks up the boys, reads them a bedtime story, and she is personally ready for bed by 9 at night. She is exhausted. She sleeps like a rock. She awakens the next day ready to do it all over again.

I then ask him about his day. He is at work early. The boys do not see him. He wakes her as he leaves. He works and arrives back home by 5:30 or 6 o'clock. He eats when they eat. Once done, he reclines in his chair and cuddles the remote until he showers and changes televisions.

I sat there waiting for him to add anything but that never happened. I was hurting for her. I reminded him of his question. Then I summarized: you don't do anything for help her.

A Working Marriage

Do you run her bath water? Iron her clothes? Rub her feet? Massage her back? I heard silence.

I suggested that he help her. Bathe a kid. Wash a dish. Unthaw the meat. Read the book at bedtime. Participate so that she is not alone. When you lighten her load, she may have the required energy to make love to you.

He said I never thought of that. I reminded him that he had been relaxing for three hours. How much time did she relax? NONE. How could she possibly have any energy leftover to please you?

Yes, she should have energy to please you on a regular basis. Can you use some of your energy to support her so that she has enough energy to want to please you? Your marriage deserves your focus. Your marriage deserves your attention. If I ask you what have you done today to invest in your marriage, what would you say? Going to work and coming home and cooking does not count. I mean what you have done specifically for the enhancement of your marriage.

When I speak to enhancing your marriage, I mean an investment in that other person. This translates differently for each person. For your husband, it may be his favorite meal or tickets to his favorite sporting event. For your wife, it will be a rose on the edge of her warm bath water or a pair of shoes you found on the page folded in that magazine on her night stand you ordered and had delivered to your office. It could be a coupon for one hour of watching whatever you want to watch for either person. It is sitting on the couch waiting on her to come home and invite her to sit with you and really listen to her, asking her engaging questions and waiting for her authentic answers. It is wearing his game jersey while cooking dinner. It is candlelight for no particular reason. It is putting the spotlight on your mate.

It is thoughts about your mate that are abnormal and above average.

It is planning a trip that one of you had always wanted. It is whatever it takes to energize your mate.

Date night needs to be regular and different and unique. Date ideas need to include events which stimulate dialogue after and during. Movies should not be considered the best thing you do. Date night needs to include a sitter or an overnight stay at a relative's home for the children.

Regular travel needs to be budgeted so that romance can always be rekindled.

How much do you know about your mate? Can you pass a quiz on your mate? If you cannot pass that quiz or if you do not know things about your mate, this is your notice that you have work to do. Knowing your mate is required.

The world has quite the view that marriages and without consequence or future issues. However, you have decided to be contrary. While your issues may seem huge, we can solve them with God's guidance and leadership, love and protection.

So, let's get started.

Changing your legacy started at 8 am. You came here. You are still here. You have some ideas about how to infuse some romance into your marriage. You have reflected on the issues of your relationships. You have even considered what you will do better when you arrive home.

You now need to re-experience the "crave" in your relationship. A craving which drives you to your spouse and keeps her on your mind all day. A craving which causes you to respond to him in all the ways he desires.

A Working Marriage

What does a new legacy look like?

A legacy which starts with a healthy, successful marriage which lasts for decades and is lived before your children and theirs.

The first element is avoiding divorce. The other elements are communication, love, respect, sexual intimacy, trust and transparency.

Decide not to be divorced. Sometimes that requires you to recall how you met and why you love him and how you fell in love. I know couples who have decided that divorce is not an option. Some of them are happy. Others are not. I hope you will be willfully engaged at the happiness level. Not just because of the kids either. Actually, being married, keep in mind one day you will be old. This is the person who has the responsibility for where you will spend any days when you are ill or in need of assisted care. Love them and treat them like you know that.

I mentioned not just for the kids. When you live this lie because we stayed married because of the kids, they have gotten divorced after twenty or twenty-five years, sometimes longer. I was in college when the parents of one of my classmates announced that they were divorcing. She was devastated. She said that this was totally unexpected. She thought that they were happy because that is the impression that they had given. She nearly failed that semester.

Children are quite perceptive. They tend to sense tension. Remaining married can be difficult but realize that if you know that you have not given your 100% effort then you need to try again until you can give it your all.

Communication is the window to all aspects of the heart, mind and soul. Say how you feel and mean what you say. Share openly and willingly what your thoughts are without prejudice or exception. Just talk to each other. Be willing to hear the hard stuff. He may need to tell you that you not working is a financial hardship. She may need to tell you that she needs more foreplay. Whatever it is, remember you love this person.

There is a part of the relationship which has become hidden to your mate. Transparency is now absent and you are hiding certain details from your mate and your marriage just changed. When did we lose the adoration for one another? When did you lose interest in your mate? When did you start hiding stuff? What changed? What does it take to regain that original transparency? Do you understand that as soon as your transparency stops, that you just sent a message to your mate? When you send that message, your mate starts to close off their transparency too? Do you realize that they can do exactly what you can do?

Transparent communication creates intimacy and breeds closeness. You need to ensure that your mate feels completely confident that they know as much or more than any other individual in your current, past and future. I dated someone once who told me that whatever someone else can tell me about you can cause damage in our relationship because I will be taken by surprise. He asked me always tell him. It has some validity. The statement means equip your mate with anything that may hurt or cause concern or considerable damage. If they know then they have power and the ability to choose.

Communication is my air. I share this in relationships because I need to share with my mate how important our conversations are. Everyone has a different communication standard. While each person may be saying communication, it can have as many different meanings and contextual connotations as there are persons in this room. His communication is checking in all day. Her communication is the details of your day including personal conversations. He does not see the need for himself to do that. She does not see a need for checking in. In our marriage, we have a problem. Each person's definition needs to be shared and fully explained and reinforced until the proper communication can be reached and shared and achieved. Until each person is completely comfortable.

Communication is your relational lifeline. It is the blood of your relationship. It needs to be practiced and rehearsed, reiterated and encouraged for the health of your relationship.

Continuing to create the legacy you desire is also deciding to avoid the stereotypes and the chatter and actively pursuing the heart of your mate. Every day is a new day to show up strong in the life of your mate. I never was a cheerleader but I completely respect what they do. They make BIG posters with the name of the school and others with the player's names. There is pride associated with that. The whole team gets excited about those posters and signs. They are made with banner paper and cheap poster paint. All of the signs are worth probably worth $10 while they create hours' worth of hype, excitement which all is defined as support.

I keep an imaginary sign with my mate's name on it. He knows it is there because when he does something great and has to face something difficult, I say that I am holding up the poster with your name on it. When I am in his presence, I hoist up my arms with an imaginary sign above my head. I smile really big too. He normally laughs. You may be thinking that it does not take all that and we are too old for that. Do as you choose; however, research shows that we as people thrive on rewards, instant gratification and support. We need to know our mate believes in us and is cheering us on. We need to give them our FULL support.

ON THE SAME TEAM

Changing the legacy means abandoning the common and the mediocre, the normal and the mundane. What are we willing to do to show your mate your love and support? What do you need your mate to do for you?

According to your goal this is the same person who you will spend the next 14,610 days with, give or take a few. If all goes according to plan, you need to do all you can to ensure that when you need depends on the likelihood that your mate is inspired and inclined to change them in a timely fashion.

Be the person's number one fan. Take the lead in their lives. Lead the touchdown dance. Be there first.

Changing the legacy means changing the perspective. It means doing the outlandish and absolutely ridiculous.

Be present daily in your marriage.

Be determined that your marriage is worth your daily investment.

Be persistent about the success of your marriage.

Be sensitive to the needs of your marriage.

Be driven to be the best friend of your mate.

Be positive about the future of your marriage.

Be diligent about the pursuit of your mate and their heart.

Be open to creative and outlandish ideas about renewing your relationship daily.

Be urgent to being self-accountable to all actions. Discard what is not good. Repeat what influences joy.

Be in love with your mate daily.

A Working Marriage

Be giving with your mate.

Be an awesome mate.

Be creative when considering igniting your marriage.

Be knowledgeable of our mate. Details solve issues.

Be conscious of your mate's fears and apprehensions.

Be faithful.

Be honest.

Be trustworthy.

Be friendly.

Be loving.

Be sacrificial.

Be the mate you prayed, hoped, wished, and yearned for so that you can have the same.

Be accountable to your mate in ways that you never have and in all the ways you always should.

Be a mate.

Be the husband.

Be the wife.

You were always supposed to be.

Then you will change the legacy in a respectable manner—one which we can all enjoy and admire.

You will learn many things today. I pray the health of your marriage. I pray the health of the heart of each of you, whether breaking or broken, I pray its healing—immediate and completely.

At the close of this lunch, you will write a love letter to your mate, detailing your new life together and the promises you will bring forward and to life in your new marriage. I challenge you to pour out your heart and give your mate what they need to press toward the next 14,610 days with you by their side.

God Bless!

Changing a Legacy, Leaving a Legacy:

A Lesson in Marriage

Love in purple,

Rev. Onedia N. Gage

A Working Marriage

IF I COULD MARRY MY BEST FRIEND

If I could marry my best friend.....

Someone I am already transparent with.

Someone whose motives I am not ever questioning.

Someone who has already heard me cry so it does not catch him by surprise. someone who loves me because I am sexy in the morning. And for the rest of the day.

Someone who tries to pay attention to my ambition.

Someone who will tell me the truth when the dress makes my butt look big and says let's go, you look great.

Or finds me something else to wear.

Someone who understands that I am comfortable in his sweats and t-shirts at home.

And understand that I will fall asleep during my own team's football game and because I do not snore it is okay.

Tell me who won when I wake up.

Someone who eats the food that I cook.

Understands when I don't.

And loves whatever I bake.

And tells me his favorite stuff.

Understands how to be surprised in a good way: gifts, notes, poetry.

A Working Marriage

Someone who reads my works and asks enough questions or offers enough feedback to be considered engaged and invested and helpful.

If only I could marry my best friend.

Table of Contents

On the Same Team: Introduction	35
Marriage Defined	39
The Honeymoon	43
Fighting Fair	45
In a White House . . .	49
Sense of Urgency	53
When All You Have is Not Enough	57
Time Management	59
On Your Terms	63
The Definition of a Snack	67
I Changed My Mind	69
Trust is Risky	71
Second Chances	77
Differing Agendas	79
What Are We Doing?	83
On the Same Team: Conclusion	85
Resources	91
Acknowledgments	93

A Working Marriage

About the Team Member   95

Book the Team Member   97

On the Same Team

A Working Marriage

A Working Marriage

On The Same Team:

A Working Marriage

Whether you have been married for one day or thirty years, marriages work if both spouses remember that you are on the same team. You chose each other. Unlike most sports teams, you chose each other. Most sports teams form based on the talents of each member, which usually are not inclusive of interpersonal skills. Whereas marriage is all about interpersonal skills.

My son was on a flag football team. He was playing as the quarterback. He handed the ball to a teammate. As soon as the teammate got the ball, my son chased him and grabbed his flag. The coach got a little upset. They lose possession of the ball again; they get in position again. My son does the same thing: "Snatch!" The same cycle repeats. This is now the third time that he takes the flag. The funniest part is that he expects a celebration but the coach throws the clipboard down while yelling, "Come here!" to all of the players. I beckoned for my son. The coach is startled and surprised. I believe that he called the timeout to speak directly to my son.

My son comes to me and says, "Yes, ma'am?" He looks sad because he is not with the team but I was convinced that I could help.

"What did the coach tell you to do?" I took a knee so that I am eye to eye with my son.

A Working Marriage

"Take the flag from the person with the ball." He was confident and confused at the same time. He wants to know why this is not working as planned. He has watched hours of football and waited his whole four-year-old life to play this game.

"Okay. Mommy wants to help you. Okay? What color are you wearing?"

"Black."

"What color is the other team wearing?"

"Red."

"Never take the flag of the person wearing your same color jersey. This means that you are on the same team. We don't take the flag from anyone on our team. Do you see the differences in the uniforms?"

"Yes, ma'am."

"Do you have any questions about what Mommy said?"

"No, ma'am."

"Do you understand what to do?"

"Yes, ma'am."

"Go out and have fun! Mommy loves you!"

"I love you too, Mommy!"

We rubbed noses and he ran to the field. The coach looks at me with a questioning expression. I held up a thumbs up.

My son went out on that field and did everything that I told him to do. They won the game. The crowd was excited. Afterwards, the coach asked me what did I say to him.

ON THE SAME TEAM

"You forgot to tell him that he could not take the flag of the person ON THE SAME TEAM. You left out those essential four words."

He lowered his head, mumbled thank you, and walked away. The message hit close to home for the coach because the coach was his father and my husband.

He had forgotten that we were on the same team as well and we were divorced the following year. This is simple enough for a four-year-old to understand, but difficult for most adults.

This marriage is only going to be successful if you remember, react, and respond; and relate with being on the same team. Your jerseys match. They are the same color, and unlike sports teams, your jersey is the same. Both jerseys have the same number.

You are a unit. You are not separate. You make decisions together. You are in debt together. You are each other's companion. You are one. You are two people who represent one decision, one team, and one brand.

You and your spouse are on the same team. That is the essential, missing element in most marriages which leads to separation, discontent, and even divorce.

On the same team lends itself to ensuring that the two of you will become one and understand the concept of how teams move together for the well-being of the team.

A Working Marriage

Marriage Defined

[18] The Lord God said, "It is not good for the man to be alone. I will make a helper suitable for him." [20] So the man gave names to all the livestock, the birds in the sky and all the wild animals.

But for Adam no suitable helper was found. [21] So the Lord God caused the man to fall into a deep sleep; and while he was sleeping, he took one of the man's ribs and then closed up the place with flesh. [22] Then the Lord God made a woman from the rib he had taken out of the man, and he brought her to the man.

[23] The man said,

"This is now bone of my bones
   and flesh of my flesh;
she shall be called 'woman,'
   for she was taken out of man."

[24] That is why a man leaves his father and mother and is united to his wife, and they become one flesh.

[25] Adam and his wife were both naked, and they felt no shame.

Genesis 2:18, 20b - 25

God created marriage. He designed a marriage with some specific freedoms and some specific boundaries. The specific boundaries include only having sex with your spouse, sacrificing for your spouse, as Christ did for the church, and being kind and compassionate to one another. God made marriage so that the wife respects and the man loves. God created marriage so that you could have a partner and an audience for your life.

A Working Marriage

Marriage is a special union. Children should only be created within the confines of marriage. Marriage has some unique behavior associated and expected.

Marriage is defined as a union between two people who at one point could not stop breathing the same air. Marriage is seen as a bond, rather traditional, led by commitment. Marriage has financial benefits, tax benefits, along with social benefits and expectations. Marriage has evolved over the years for cultural reasons and societal norms. The main theme of marriage is there is one union which needs to be respected and honored, maintained and nurtured, promoted and provocative. Marriage requires your energy and enthusiasm, love and commitment, loyalty and persistence. What are you giving to your marriage? Is your attitude and disposition toward your relationship positive, even when the climate of the relationship may range from partly cloudy to torrential downpour? Keep in mind that your attitude will make the difference in the success or demise of your relationship.

Marriage is an active organ. It can't be treated like a stagnant or static element. Marriage requires care and nurture such that it may live. Similar to a plant or your body where water and food are required to grow and live, time and attention are required for the health and welfare of a great marriage.

Conversely, your mate is not simply the maid, handyman, or sex partner: they are your partner in the relationship.

On The Same Team

A Working Marriage

The Honeymoon

Bliss! You married your best friend, your soulmate, your high school or college sweetheart. You have known the best and maybe the worst about the other person.

The honeymoon is how long the bliss lasts. When the bliss starts to end, what do you do? You have started to merge money and bills and you are finding out that there are layers to that onion. The honeymoon is the fairytale and it may not be the most realistic version of yourself and that person. Keep in mind that we are imagining that the bliss will continue.

That is not realistic, however, what is realistic is that we will experience change in the other person as well as ourselves. The honeymoon is a protected space because all parties are on their best behavior–time is respected and honored, feelings are considered; respect is fluent and fluid. These components are essential to the success of the actual marriage.

The honeymoon is also about making great memories, which you will need when times become tough, or stagnant. Your relationship may face challenges. Your memories are designed to provide a soft place to land and linger because you will need them to motivate and to remind you why you are together.

Keep that in mind. The honeymoon is the best of times.

A Working Marriage

During the honeymoon: Laugh. Play. Create. Support. Meet each other's needs.

The challenge is keeping the honeymoon alive. The process is based on investment. What does that investment look like? What is required? Can you sustain what you initiated?

These affirmative questions increase the probability that you are able to prolong the honeymoon. When the honeymoon subsides, the real work begins. We do not actually look forward to that space.

On The Same Team

A Working Marriage

On The Same Team

Fighting Fair

> *When you pick a fight, pick one which leads you to loving another person greater than you ever thought possible, better than they think they deserve, and more extravagantly than is even reasonable. Life is too short for anything else. You deserved to be loved at that level and you deserve to love at that same level of extravagance!*

Most people fight but they rarely fight fairly. You and your mate may fight, but the challenge is how to fight fairly and so that you are able to maintain your relationship once the fight is done.

The result of the fight needs to be a solution where both parties are satisfied. Fighting if they are also means that each person is heard and each person gets a voice in the matter. Fighting fair also means that no one is lying about the matter(s) at hand.

There are some essential pieces to fighting fairly; here they are: truth, trust, and truce.

Tell the truth. This is the problem with most people - the lies that you tell yourself and others. Tell the actual truth. It is better to share the truth than it is to lie. Although it is easier to lie, that leads to more damage and more lies. Lies hurt most of the time more than the truth does. Why is telling the truth so hard? This answer is one which varies from person to person, but the bottom line is that the lies are based on fear. Lies are based on the fear of the consequences of the truth. Lies destroy trust and confidence. Lies erode the foundation of that relationship. Lies negate love. You cannot love and lie to the same person.

What does it require to be able to tell the truth? What does it mean to tell the truth? What is so bad about the truth? When will you be able to tell the truth? Soon enough to save your relationship? If the truth cannot be repeated, then why is it a reality?

There is an old adage which states what is good for the goose is good for the gander. That is supported by doing unto others what you would have them do unto you. If you can't tell anyone, then you shouldn't do it. Who wants to love someone who is deceitful?

Truth leads to trust. What can your mate trust you with? What don't they trust you with? What should your mate trust you with? What did you do to earn the trust of your mate? Have you done anything to ruin that trust? Trust is being able to know what you hear is factual, what you see is factual, and what you do is authentic.

Lying and cheating is the usual mechanism by which trust is destroyed. The mate will ask what did she/he did to deserve this treatment. The fact is that they did not do anything and they cannot stop you at all. Hundreds of studies have been done about cheating and the reasons why and the methods to prevent it. There is no one reason for cheating and lying.

Fighting fair is the key to resolve issues within your relationship. Key one to fighting fair is listening. Listening to your mate is the most important part to solving your issues. What are the actual issues? What is the real issue? Sometimes the fight is the decoy for the real issue. One of the arguments that leads to the need of a decoy is not wanting to face the actual issues. The key to listening is to do that: listen. Don't talk. Just listen. Don't interrupt. Use a notebook to take notes of questions that you think of while your mate is talking. Don't interrupt. I cannot say this enough: just listen.

LISTEN.

When they are done talking, then ask some questions about what they need and what they mean. What is hurting him or her? What does she or he need or want?

A Working Marriage

The key will also be what is she/he not sharing. The communication will start the sorting of issues which have been making a negative impact on your relationship. After the questions, you will then need to offer your full remorse for what the problems are.

Next, make an offer of solution. What is the remedy for those problems? What can you do to grow closer to your mate? What happens when you offer your authentic intimacy to your mate? Your mate has needs that you want to meet but you don't know exactly what they are - find out. Do something about it.

Fighting fair does not mean that you need to win. You need to be okay with reaching a resolve, even if you don't actually have a win.

Your home and other environments need peace so that you and your mate can coexist in a safe place and become closer.

Fighting fair is a safe place for both of you to share your truths and find a solution for the issues that you all have. Fighting fair involves understanding the actual issues and how to reach an amicable solution. When this happens, then you will be excited to work through the details of your lives - both good and bad.

On The Same Team

A Working Marriage

In a White House . . .

If we recall the 1980s and the television shows about family, we may recall that most of these homes were white. This became the attachment to the ideal marriage and the definition of the dream of the perfect family. The White House also is depicted with a white picket fence. In this fairytale depiction, we do not know the status of the contentment or joy in that family which resides behind those closed doors.

Marriage is sacred so are its aspects, secrets which other people may never know. That door which closes behind you when you go inside is the place where you live the dreams that you have always had.

The façade of the White House does not equate to happiness or marital bliss or marital longevity. It merely means that there was a home purchase that was white. It means that as a couple you will work harder at marriage than you have at anything in your life ever. The inside of that home needs to be a place of retreat. Your home needs to be your sanctuary — your place of peace. There are some rules regarding marriage.

1. Your home is your place of peace. Treat it as such. Home is where you rest and recharge, revive and refresh. It is time to reunite with your mate.

2. Your home is your sanctuary. It is a place where you shut out the world and leave your troubles at the curb. It is a place where the sign which reads 'do not disturb' hangs on the door at all times.

3. Your home is your safe place. It is where you can put your stuff down and where you can solve all of your problems. It is your safe haven where secrets are protected. Your mate will be held sacred by you as well.

4. Be honest. With your mate. About your life, issues, and dreams. When you come home and your spouse asks you how your day was, tell the truth. Please don't use the words 'fine' and 'okay.' Please don't use those words which create distance, distrust, and doubt. Your mate knows. And cares. About what is wrong with you, so remember that your mate is your first supporter and cheerleader. Please share and do not make him or her beg to be your safe place to land.

5. Commit to be peaceful at home. Listen before judging. Observe before concluding. Remember that your mate is not the enemy. Your mate is your strategy partner. This is the person who tells you that your idea needs work or that your idea will ensure that you will be successful.

6. Give your mate your full attention at home. You need that affirmation from each other. When you come home are you on the phone? Should you get off the phone before entering the house? If not, how long will you be on the phone? Is this different depending on who you're talking on the phone with?

7. Honor each other's opinions and space. You are still a person while working toward the oneness that you are working to create. You still have an opinion and a voice

in your mate's life and your relationship. Use it to undergird and uplift your mate. Please don't use your experience and knowledge to make your spouse feel less than. What you know, you're obligated to share with your mate because their success matters to you and affects you. So conversely, you will suffer when she/he suffers because of what they don't know and what they cannot use to be successful.

8. Your home should feel like love when you both enter. Work hard at that at all times.

9. Keep your home clean. Both of you. This is the responsibility of both parties.

10. Keep your home smelling fresh and inviting. The smells of aromatherapy are healthy for your spirit. The aroma is soothing and rejuvenating.

11. Honor each other's expectations and homegrown traditions, inclusive of any pet peeves.

Above all else, keep the focus on your mate and the growth, maturation, and the closeness of this relationship.

In the white house with the picket fence, there needs to be honor and praise, celebrations and traditions, accountability and trust. You will experience other feelings as well, so be open to really letting your guard down and authentically letting your mate into your heart and mind and life.

Protect your home! At all costs! Even if it is from yourself!

A Working Marriage

ON THE SAME TEAM

Sense of Urgency

On the same team requires a strong sense of urgency. Since the urgency means that you respond to your mate and their real time, not your 'real whenever you feel like it time.' Your life is busy and complicated, awkward and successful, hectic and fulfilling. However, your mate is first before all of that. Support and safety is sustained through responsiveness to each other's needs and desires.

When you delay taking action when your mate request something, how does that make him or her feel? Consider what would happen if you felt that you were not only not first, but more like fifth? You figure this out because he fixes his mom's broken everything before he fixes your anything. You also cannot call a repair person. When you realize that you have no influence in your mate's life, then what will you do and how does that feel? The sense of urgency is critical and necessary because in you lies a source of comfort and strength for your mate.

The example of repairs is one simple example. This extends into every aspect of your lives together. This sense of urgency includes sex, travel, food preparation, and all other areas of your lives.

Marriage is about being an audience to your mate. This marriage is for your personal satisfaction and gratification. Your mate is your partner – in almost all things.

A Working Marriage

There will be recommendations from other married couples, and even some divorced persons that will state that you should not do EVERYTHING together. They may advise you not to open a business together and other such advice, but the reality is you have to make your own choices. These decisions will need to be made using all of the necessary data. This and any decisions that are made for your marriage need to be made with honesty and the purest of intentions. And with a sense of urgency.

Your mate and your relationship deserve and require your attention with zeal, fervor, and urgency.

Sense of urgency may seem like a processing issue for the other person but the reality is that although you may have never used this exact lens, this is the time to examine the concept using the lens so that you can see the need to see it. Your attention to your mate is quite important. Your attention to their needs is directly tied to your evaluation of their self-esteem and self-worth. If you consider the concept, then you will realize that your mate may place value on events and behavior that no one else can make sense of. It could be the quirkiest detail but it's also attached to the person that you love, or in love with, and are married to, so it does not matter how weird their feelings are. They are your responsibility and so are their feelings and the rest of their details. No matter what.

Listen to your mate. Take action and do what they need and this work is reciprocal. Reciprocity is also key to the health of the relationship. Your goal is to outdo the other person. This sense of urgency is the responsibility of both parties. Communication is helpful in making the sense of urgency easier to understand and navigate.

There is a village that was not able to eat. The spoons were too long and they could feed themselves because they could not turn the spoons around while keeping the food on the spoon. This lasted for several weeks. One day, a village member decided to feed another village member with the spoon. The village member who received the food was so excited that she was finally able to eat. Because this worked, she fed the village member who fed her. While they were enjoying their food, the other village members started doing the same. The community started working together and was able to accomplish more than they ever had individually. There is a message here for marriages. This is the essence of being on the same team.

A Working Marriage

When All You Have Is Not Enough

There are people who get married but are also critics of their same mate and relationships. This is quite unfortunate because you thought that you marry someone who had your best interest at heart.

Consider why you wanted to marry and be married and what you thought that marriage would be like. How did you reach that imagery? What event(s) or person(s) shaped your marital desires and your idea(s) of what marriage would be like? What is required to reach that definition of marriage? What happens when you don't reach that expectation? How do you incorporate your definition and desires with your mate in order to reach a mutually satisfying marriage?

What happens when all that you have is not enough to keep your mate engaged? Emotionally healthy? Focused on you and your relationship? What happens when you don't get what you were promised and what you bargained for? What will you do now? Next?

Most of us would just quit. Quitting is defined as divorce, infidelity, or anything that removes your focus from the marital relationship. We cannot afford to quit. Your marriage deserves your fight.

A Working Marriage

First, make sure that you are not the problem in the relationship. So, having said that, what are you doing to equip your mate to be successful with you? This is not a job; you are not at work. This is your partner! If your marriage fails, then you are a participant in that failure so, it is also yours. It is never clear about what you need because we are all ever evolving. As you consider what you need in your relationship, remember that you are tasked with making sure that your mate has a detailed road map of you because you are their person.

Second, your goal in a relationship is to keep your relationship free from attack. The only way to do that is to equip your mate. The other way to do that is to also communicate to your mate what your needs, goals, and expectations are. The other part is to make sure that you are sharing your innermost thoughts, needs, and feelings.

Why don't you feel that you are enough? Did you decide that you weren't enough or did your mate say that?

On The Same Team

A Working Marriage

Time Management

Contrary to the myth, we all have 24 hours a day, 7 days a week, and 365 days each year. The difference is what you do with that time. Are you judicious over that time? Do you make excuses about the misuse of your time?

What time do you require of your mate? Do you need one hour each day? Do you need the whole weekend? Do you just need special occasions? Do you need to attend every concert? Do you need to travel on all holidays? Do you just want a few hours each week?

Recall that you are married to this person and we are discussing a limited time and a scheduled time for your spouse. This is the person that you're supposed to do everything with and spend all of your time with.

The feelings of your mate need to be considered when your mate does not get the time that they desire. What does your mate think about your absence? What your mate thinks about your absence is critically important. When you found time to visit your friends to watch a football game almost all day but you cannot seem to avail yourself for a 90-minute lunch, there may be some hurt feelings and some pending conversations and consequences. When that time is spent on something else extracurricular such as an affair, this will bring issues to your relationship. This is the hardest part of the relationship — you chose to spend your time with someone else who you purposely made time for. How is that going to feel? How will you feel if that was you? But you don't believe that she will do that to you? Why would you risk such a horrific situation?

Give your mate the time that they need. You got married because you once desired and even craved that time together. The time renews and rejuvenates this relationship — keeps it new and desirable. The time that a relationship need should be planned and spontaneous. This is a necessary commitment and obligation for every relationship because each relationship started with time and attention. This is the one concept which is not measurable or immediately recognizable.

Time needs to be protected and cherished. Time isn't something that you can create or get back or make up for. Time is your insurance against infidelity or distance, divisiveness or disinterest, and whatever other reasons for divorce and separation exist.

Consider your future self. Does your future self wish for your 'former' relationships? As we consider the time, there is no one that can say that they did not wish for more time with their spouses with plenty of regret for the time that they misused and squandered. Time is precious and while it's often taken for granted, attempt to be someone that does not do that.

Schedule date night. Do different activities. Try activities that are free as well as ticketed events that cost hundreds. Budget is important in some cases.

Schedule vacations. From the free to the outlandish. Where is your dream travel list? Do the things you never considered before. Get your passports if you do not already have them.

Use your time wisely. Give your time to your mate willingly. Your mate deserves your best. Balance your time. Work. Play. Marriage. Family. Those percentages will change daily but no matter the split, marriage comes first. Your mate will be the longest standing person in your life. Protect your marriage with all that you have. Time is critical. Time is the oxygen that many relationships need. If you're not spending time together, then you are not growing closer together as a couple. The time that you spend together is critical for the intimacy that you need to sustain the relationship.

Without oxygen, you will die. Without time, so will your relationship.

A family calendar helps with keeping track and making plans. Calendar invites serve as a placeholder and reminder. This ensures that you are not double booked and that you do not forget what you have planned.

What needs to happen for you to crave your mate again? There were countless hours that you two spent together and now somehow you could avoid your mate if the opportunity presents itself. There are moments that you were so close to each other

A Working Marriage

that you cannot tell when one of you starts and the other one of you ends.

Time management is essential to the success of the relationship as it is in other aspects of your life. Your time management is a part of the respect for your relationship.

Spend your time with such respect that your mate never questions your commitment or intentions.

On The Same Team

A Working Marriage

On Your Terms

We all have preferences and habits, mannerisms and idiosyncrasies. These details are the distinguishing parts of what makes us unique. In those details, what is most evident? How do those details make a difference in your relationship?

If you relate to the phrase 'my way or the highway,' then your mate is in trouble. What are your terms when you refer to that relationship? Some of us are better than others at compromise. But do understand that everyone has a boundary line, a line in the sand, a point of no return, and some non-negotiables. Please know that about yourself and your mate.

So, let's talk terms. If you go to buy a car or home – anything where the interest rate is a detail, then you want the lowest possible rate and the best amount of months. If you don't like the interest rate or the other stipulations, then it is likely that you will leave without that vehicle or you will select another mortgage company for that home purchase. The rate also depends on your credit score. The higher your score, the better your interest rate so it is reasonable to say that if your credit score is in the 400s, then your rate will be the in the teens, for example 14% or higher. This will fluctuate based on the product that you are purchasing but overall, that is a relationship of those factors.

Now, consider a relationship. You can do certain things based on your credit – your other areas which are great lets you get away

A Working Marriage

with other things which would otherwise not be acceptable. Let's be specific if you are late but you make great meals and make a great home, then your mate makes a concession for you. So, what happens when your meals are not so great and your house is not as well kept? There is the credit and the allowances of the relationship. What do you have good credit for and what will it yield you high interest which equates to low tolerance?

This is all measured differently from person to person and from relationship to relationship. What one woman is okay with, another woman will leave you because of it. The same applies to men. The measurement and criteria are different and sometimes without notice; usually without an announcement or rationale being provided.

What can you get away with? No sex? No meals cooked? No laundry? Stay out all night? Cheating? Having a medical procedure which prevents you from being able to conceive? And your spouse does not agree, so definitely does not know? Lending money without a discussion? Spending above a certain amount of money without a discussion? What can your relationships sustain? Why would you want to put your relationship through that? What would it cost you because you cannot respect the boundaries of your relationship? If you are willing to violate the nature of the relationship, then why are you in that relationship?

Relationships are supposed to be safe places. Relationships are a place where you're able to be vulnerable. When you cannot trust your mate and you cannot find peace at home because you can't take off your mask; you cannot relax your representative; all because your mate favors the outside world and sometimes poses as and represents the enemy, the future of your relationship can topple with the force of air that one uses a cool hot food on the end of a fork.

Do you want to be married? If so, then put your terms in the delete box. Stop making it hard to be in a relationship with you.

Consider that your terms are not conducive to the health of your mate. The unrealistic, unrelenting terms make you appear like an opportunist because you are taking advantage of the desire to love you but will hurt another person with these terms. These difficult moments within the relationship strain the relationship as well as creates distance with your mate.

The terms were developed as a defense mechanism. These terms also create tension and possibly dissension and division with your relationship. The problem then is that one of you is only staying because there are benefits.

When you or your mate are only staying together because of 'something' rather than love is a business deal not a relationship.

Relationships should be based on wanting the other person. Rather than needing the accessories of the other person, such as sex, money, property, status, or whatever else is a tangible or intangible element that adds value to your life that you would otherwise not have.

A Working Marriage

On your terms is a selfish place where you neglect the needs and desires of your mate for selfish and narcissistic purposes. Put them to the side. Suspend your rules and your terms. Consider your mate's needs and start to intertwine together, so that you can make a better relationship.

That is the definition of being on the same team.

On The Same Team

A Working Marriage

ON THE SAME TEAM

The Definition of a Snack

Him: "I want a snack."

Her: "Okay. What do you want?"

Him: "I was thinking about a burger, fries, and a milkshake."

Her: "That is NOT a snack. That is a full course meal."

Him: "To you."

What is the definition of a snack? His definition? Her definition? Whether they are the same or not, they are still together.

Among the decisions that a couple makes on a daily basis, this may not be at the top of the list, it is of importance. It is about an understanding—one that every couple needs to reach.

Why are definitions necessary? You need to be starting at the same place of understanding. If you don't understand each other, then you ask each other what 'it' means. Then ask what else 'it' means. Sometimes, more often than not, there are more than obvious reasons for actions and there could be several 'whys.'

Now, this is where caution becomes important because you don't want to be the withholder of the information. Or the person who withholds the 'why' and never discloses the 'it.'

A Working Marriage

The couple had an aha moment–each one had a revelation. She expanded her understanding of the definition of a snack. He learned how to explain.

Let this be the reason for the rest of us. What if you expanded your understanding and actually started to explain? What transforms that relationship? These are the aspects that make the difference in actual great relationships. Be the person that you desire in a relationship so that both parties can be satisfied and happy in the relationship.

The definition of what the other person needs is important to that individual. Use that lens to make all of your decisions. Your mate deserves the best of you. In turn, you deserve the best of them. This cyclical reciprocity is how couples thrive, not just survive. The circular reciprocity is the base of all great partnerships, and relationships. The couples who do this authentically are the couples who sustain the race and continue the journey no matter what the obstacles present.

Discussing the definition of a snack is part of being on the same team. Full disclosure and transparency are critical to the success of wearing the same jersey.

On The Same Team

A Working Marriage

On The Same Team

I Changed My Mind

This phrase is quite valuable when considering the communication which would have made life easier. When you change YOUR mind or make a different decision than previously expected, then you should share that new direction/decision immediately. YOUR decision affects the other person as well. You are a team. Your decisions affect another person, possibly some children, and other family members. This is not an easy concept to consider. Your every move, mood, thought, and dream affects other people–the people that you claim to love and those you are in love with and love you.

Changes are okay if they are able to help the entire family and not impose hurt and harm. People need time to process the changes within this life. Consider that you decide to buy a car. If it takes four days for you to decide on a car, then you need to offer your spouse at least four days in order to process that decision and start to acclimate to that change. Sometimes the decisions are harder than buying a car. Other decisions include not returning to work after childbirth, starting a business without consent using a joint savings account, changing careers with less money, planning trips without building consensus first, among other examples. These events are able to break a relationship. These events can bring your relationship to its knees. These events when handled incorrectly can be the start of the statistic of divorce. Changing your mind as well as making decisions without a consensus and agreement from your mate versus a huge deal breaker for most couples.

A Working Marriage

What can you do about being on the same team? About changing your mind but neglecting communication with your mate.

This is not about asking permission. There was a conference where married women were discussing telling their husbands about buying a dress or several. One attendee asked why did she need to consult her husband about buying a dress and she works daily.

The onslaught of advice was overwhelming. Those women had lots of advice. The advice was overwhelming. They had every angle on how the basis of the communication and how this communication effects your overall relationship. People are married to people who they can trust, who they can believe in, and who they can communicate with.

Because of those needs, and even requirements, when you change any of those, you need to share that with your partner. Transparency is a building block for your relationship. The lack of communication and transparency leads to a disrupted relationship.

Being on the same team means that you do all of what is mentioned in this chapter. Being on the same team means that you make every effort to share, or even over share so that you will be on the same page.

ON THE SAME TEAM

A Working Marriage

Trust Is Risky

There are risks in this life, especially in relationships. This is a relationship that you chose. You should be able to trust and to be trusted. So why is this so hard to do? Why exactly are we hard to trust? Lack of trust is due to lies, nondisclosures, and non-truths. This lack of trust is also not being dependable with your word and your whereabouts.

A relationship, a marriage is the ultimate commitment between two people and is also an extension into the lives of others. This new life as a married couple includes sharing toothpaste, toilet paper, door handles, windows, refrigerators, drawers, shelves, and some Yeti cups. A person is trusting you and you are trusting the other party. That is what you agreed to: TRUST.

Trust means that you will believe what your mate says and does, you will believe their words and whereabouts. And that is mutual.

Trust: Unequivocally resting the weight of who you are at the disposal of another. This requires a fierce transparency that most people fail at in general.

Consider what it costs to share EVERYTHING with your mate regardless of what it will do; it could possibly hurt that mate.

A Working Marriage

There have been conversations where you have lied. What are the consequences of that lie? What can you do to stop lying? Why is sharing the truth so hard?

Gage has a theory that if you had better self-esteem, then the lies would not be created and shared. Imagine that you don't do things which offer you the opportunity to need to lie.

Stop doing things that make you have to lie in order to explain your actions, thoughts, and whereabouts.

Just stop engaging in activities that force you to lie. Are those shoes new? No, they have been at the back of the closet. That is a lie. Tell him that your day was terrible and these new shoes made you feel better. Or whatever your reason was for buying shoes that were not in your budget or breaks an agreement that you made.

Trust is something that should be easy to maintain. Don't you want your mate to trust you? Don't you want your mate to authentically believe you?

Don't lie.

Don't break your covenant.

Don't break your promises.

Don't hide your purchases.

ON THE SAME TEAM

Don't disappear.

Don't share what belongs to your mate with someone else.

Don't cheat.

Don't hide your feelings.

Don't go on trips with someone that is not your mate.

Don't share your business with others.

Don't forget important days and dates.

Don't forget to keep your mate's secrets.

Keep your mate's heart safe.

Remember to tell your mate everything that you tell others. No one should know something that your mate does not know.

Don't let your mate down.

Don't disappoint your mate.

Don't do things that will discourage your mate.

Trust is hard to develop. Once developed, it is hard to sustain. Trust is harder to recreate once it is destroyed. Do you really want to destroy the trust of your mate? Because you are being secretive or disloyal or lying?

Guard your trust. Guard your relationship. Guard your covenant. Guard all of the components of your marriage. Trust is sacred. It is what you are known for. Trust is critical for the longevity of your relationship.

A Working Marriage

Let's talk about a particular married couple. He travels twice a year with another woman. She goes to bed at 8PM. He has had several affairs. She does not seem to care. They are not learning from each other. They both have been unemployed. They have supported each other through children and child support and visitation denial.

Whatever the details of their relationship do not matter, what matters is that they decided that to stay.

Does she trust him? No one knows but who wants to be in that type of relationship. Most people don't. What kind of relationship do you want? Consider the climate of your relationship when you have cheated or lied or disrupted the climate enough.

What is important about your relationship? Is it worth discarding the trust that you have developed? Is your mate worth your trust? Your truth? Your transparency? Your authentic self? Is your mate worth your whole self? Wasn't your mate worth it when you engaged in that relationship?

Trust is based on a promise and potential. Plenty of people break promises and fully miss their potential. Trust is risky. TRUST is hard to come by and is hard to sustain.

What do you want to give your mate and what do you want from your mate? Whatever the issues are, do EVERYTHING that you can do ensure that your word means the world to your mate and a word that you can absolutely be proud of.

Can you put your phone in the palm of your mate's hand with the password entered and the phone unlocked? Can you talk on speaker phone to EVERYONE who calls you on the phone? Can you sit with all of your friends in the presence of your mate? If you can't answer those questions in the affirmative, then you need to change your behavior. Earning the trust of your mate is your top priority.

Trust can be ruined because of your actions. So clean them up.

Be present in your relationship. Give your mate what she/he needs to be comfortable in the relationship so that they can thrive and love you as he/she should.

Trust is to be protected. Nothing is worth more. If it is not, then walk away. Leave your mate with some dignity and self-esteem.

A Working Marriage

Second Chances

A second chance. What is a second chance? Why will you need a second chance? Why would you need to offer your mate a second chance?

Forgiveness in a relationship is essential. But we do not need to consider forgiveness if we do not do anything that requires forgiveness.

Stop making mistakes which cause you to need a second chance and forgiveness.

Easier said than done? Maybe, but not so much. If you need a second chance, then please take that opportunity seriously. It is in poor taste not to take the second chance seriously. Please consider that someone put aside their pride in order to reconcile with you. If you are the beneficiary of an authentic second chance, then make sure that you don't make your mate look foolish for attempting to reconcile and rehabilitate your relationship.

Please consider that you have done something that you would not have tolerated, and now you need some grace. Would you have extended that same grace?

A Working Marriage

Please consider all of those factors when you decide to make a decision to violate the tenants of your marriage.

Second chances are precious. Hopefully, you will never need a second chance. Hopefully, you will never have to offer a second chance.

On The Same Team

A Working Marriage

ON THE SAME TEAM

Differing Agendas

Most couples dream of being a power couple. That couple who walks into rooms and everyone looks in their direction. The room was waiting on them to appear so they could see what they were wearing. Is that you? Are you the power couple or do you want to be that couple? Do both of you want the same thing?

There are people who get married for different reasons, some so different that from the outside, no one can even understand why that union even made sense. If it looks bad from a distance, then it is terrible up close.

Let's consider a case study of a couple. She is a city-bred woman who is well educated. She is a product of divorced parents. She was fiercely independent, and an overachiever to some. intellectually savvy. Popular.

He is from a small, rural town. A country boy. Not city savvy. Limited educational experiences. His parents stayed married until his father died. He needs other people and he needs consistent affirmation. Somewhat popular.

They are so different and they were married, however their marriage did not last. Part of it was because of differing agendas and priorities. You may know this couple. You may be this couple or have been this couple in a previous relationship.

A Working Marriage

She wanted to have two children naturally and adopt a third. He did not want to adopt a child, so she conceded and they did not adopt a child. She wanted to stay home after she had their child, but he didn't want her to do so. She wanted to move within the suburbs but he already own the land so that's where they built a house.

Then the tides turned, she stayed at home after the second child was born and then the climate changed. He didn't realize that this would have changed the trajectory of their relationship. She felt that her mate did not respect her so moving forward she stopped investing in him and transitioned to herself and then her children. He was not social like she was so they didn't go to the same events nor have the same friends.

The point here is that the couple can be attracted to each other and still be unequally yoked. What is on your agenda? How do you decide if your agendas match? What happens when they don't?

Let's start with why did you get married? Love? Or something else? A woman said once that love was not the only reason to marry. How many people are actually doing that?

How do you know when you're married for love and the other person married because of corporate ties, financial stability, family obligation to another wealthy family, in exchange for debt, and other similar situations.

ON THE SAME TEAM

Can you imagine getting married to someone that you love but you find out that they do not love you in return? How do you think arranged marriages feel? How can you survive this? What can you do if that is not your desire? How do you overcome that process? What questions should you have asked in order to make sure that you were getting married for the same reasons? What happens if you go ask your mate why she or he married you? What is your answer? Has anything changed about why you married this person? Would you marry that same person now? Consider why or why not. Consider that the person is asking the same question so they are answering that question as well.

What can you do to align these agendas? Not just the reasons for marriage but daily items. These include should we move for careers, how to raise children, what to buy or not to buy, and what to invest in. These are a few of the topics where alignment is challenged.

Be considerate of the agenda of the other person as they are of your agenda.

A Working Marriage

What Are We Doing

Every marriage has challenges and victories. The goal is to have the victories to be so special and so powerful that the victories outweigh the challenges. So, what are we doing? In this life? In this marriage? What does this marriage require so that you can make it to a decade? If that is the first decade or the fourth decade?

Do you need a refresher for the reconnection that you need? Have you considered a retreat? Have you considered counseling? What are your objectives for your marriage? To stay married? To increase the communication? To increase the chemistry? To increase the intimacy? To increase the understanding of each other? To become one?

There is danger in assuring that you and your mate are in sync on the next level for the relationship. So, consider having that discussion. Marriage brings people and their families together. This union is remarkable phenom which was designed for bliss and excitement, joy and love, companionship and fulfillment but we have to contribute to this union for its sustainment.

We pray against divorce and disconnect. This is a tragic end to what was designed to be the best thing that ever happened to you.

A Working Marriage

In 1990, a young lady was sitting at her college desk in tears because her parents were going to divorce after 25 years of marriage. she was devastated. When her college friends ask her about it, she said that she was totally surprised - now devastated.

Consider carefully the effect on others when you contemplate this option. This has to be the final option. Be careful to consider the requests of your mate so, that you can return to the feeling that got you into this marriage in the first place. Start to court again. Go on dates. Do screen-free dates. Travel more. Seek advice from a counselor. This is for everyone, not only for couples considering divorce.

The goal is for your marriage to remain a marriage, preferably healthy and whole. Spend the same time on your relationship that you spend on your job or your business that is successful.

On The Same Team

A Working Marriage

On The Same Team

My son was on a flag football team. He was playing as the quarterback. He handed the ball to a teammate. As soon as the teammate got the ball, my son chased him and grabbed his flag. The coach gets a little upset. They lose possession of the ball but got the ball back, they get in position again. My son does the same thing: "snatch." The same cycle repeats. This is now the third time that he takes the flag. The funniest part is that he expects a celebration but the coach throws the clipboard down while yelling, "Come here!" to all of the players. I beckon for my son. The coach is startled and surprised. I believe that he called the timeout to speak directly to my son.

My son comes to me and says, "Yes, ma'am?" He looks sad because he is not with the team but I was convinced that I could help.

"What did the coach tell you to do?" I am eye to eye with my son.

"Take the flag from the person with the ball." He was confident and confused at the same time. He wants to know why this is not working as planned. He has watched hours of football and waited his whole four-year-old life to play this game.

"Okay. Mommy wants to help you. Okay? What color are you wearing?"

"Black."

"What color is the other team wearing?"

"Red."

A Working Marriage

"Never take the flag of the person wearing your same color jersey. This means that you are on the same team. We don't take the flag from anyone on our team. Do you see the differences in the uniforms?"

"Yes, ma'am."

"Do you have any questions about what Mommy said?"

"No, ma'am."

"Do you understand what to do?"

"Yes, ma'am."

"Go out and have fun! Mommy loves you!"

"I love you too, Mommy!"

We rubbed noses and he ran to the field. The coach looks at me with a questioning expression. I held up a thumbs up.

The timeout is over so he meets his team. They got into the formation. They start to play. First play successful. Touchdown.

They did it four more times.

When the game was over, they had won the game. He was awarded the MVP award. They celebrated, passed out snacks, and packed up to leave.

The coach came over to me and asked me what I said to his quarterback.

My response was, "I told my son not to take the flag of someone who is on the same team."

The coach hung his head.

"You left off the four most important words: On the Same Team."

ON THE SAME TEAM

He was speechless. When he walked away, he felt differently than I did about the encounter, but both were ever changed.

That incident led to the title of this book.

Can you imagine watching an NBA basketball game and the home team passes the ball to the other team intentionally? That would seem odd and some of the other players will be angry because that sabotages the plan of being on the same team.

Being on the same team means that you are totally supportive of each other. It's the bond between you that causes others, including your children, to say that we will not bother that couple because everyone knows that they are a real couple, not to be disturbed by drama and nonsense.

The worst thing ever is to feel that your mate does not support you in your decisions or your ventures. Being on the same team means that you actually have each other's back. It means that you believe in each other. It also means that you will cooperate with one another.

In the movie, 'Love and Basketball,' Monica, the main character, says to her counterpart, "I'll play you for your heart." Her 'all in' challenge was clear for him. If he was unclear, then she made it clearer for him. "I need and want you." That is a huge step. This is not for the faint at heart. The characters of Love and Basketball we're very familiar with team. They were both basketball players. They completely depended on their teams. They had to work to depend on each other. They eventually

A Working Marriage

reunited and then married. This is a great love story. Please take time to make your own.

Being a unit, being a team, being one, being on the same page is the ultimate goal. The prize in every relationship is the reciprocity of the love and care the develops from the relationship's chemistry.

There is an additional point to this as well. Do you want to be 'needed' or 'wanted'? There is a definite split on this matter however, you should consider the following: if someone wants you, there's an authentic energy that is created from that behavior. Relationships that are developed from want last longer and has a different sustainment factor than a relationship based on need. In the 'want' relationship, everyone wants to be there.

In the 'need' relationship, someone is dependent on another person. That need is like an obligation, rather than a desire. What happens when that person no longer needs you? What happens when one person no longer wants to fulfill that need? What happens when you feel like a hostage because of that need? What does it mean when you do not have any individual freedom because of that need? What happens when you start to resent and mistreat the other person because of that need?

At any rate, on the same team is the goal of any relationship but it's imperative in any marriage. This is the only way to survive decades with you with each other that you each signed up for.

On the Same Team!

A Working Marriage

Resources

The Five Love Languages by Dr. Gary Chapman
Married Roommates by Allen Wagner
The Sex-Starved Marriage: A Couple's Guide to Boosting Their Marriage Libido
Woulda. Coulda. Shoulda.: A Divorce Coach's Guide to Staying Married by Jennifer Hurvitz
I Love You But I Don't Trust You by Mira Kirshenbaum
Talk to Me Like I am Someone You Love by Nancy Dreyfus
From Two to One: The Notebook for the Christian Couple by Minister Onedia N. Gage
Getting Away to Get It Together by Bill and Carolyn Wellons
The Love Dare by Alex and Stephen Kendrick
Saving Your Marriage Before It Starts by Drs. Les and Leslie Parrott
Questions Couples Ask by Drs. Les and Leslie Parrott
Powerful Promises for Every Couple by Jim and Elizabeth George
The Christian Husband by Bob Lepine
Kingdom Man by Tony Evans
Kingdom Woman by Tony Evans
The Power of a Praying Wife by Stormie Omartian
The Power of a Praying Husband by Stormie Omartian
The Power of Prayer to Change Your Marriage by Stormie Omartian
The Excellent Wife by Martha Peace
The Excellent Husband by Martha Peace
40 Unforgettable Dates with Your Mate by Dr. Gary and Barbara Rosberg
When God Writes Your Love Story by Eric and Leslie Ludy
Love and Respect by Emerson Eggerichs

Movies
The Longest Ride
The Story of Us
We Bought a Zoo
Hope Springs
Best Man Holiday

A Working Marriage

Shall We Dance
Jerry MacGuire
It's Complicated
Fireproof
Sweet Home Alabama
The Women
Mr. & Mrs. Smith
The Notebook
War Room
Jumping the Broom
Something to Talk About
The Devil Loves Prada
A Thousand Words
Love and Basketball
The Blind Side
50 Shades Darker
Creed 2
The Other Woman
Up Close & Personal
The Vow

Acknowledgements

God, thank You for Your plans for me. Thank You for ***On the Same Team,*** and choosing me to complete Your project. I just want to please You, God. Thank You for continuing to anoint me and to invest in me and my gifts, which keep surprising me. Thank You for loving and forgiving me.

Jordan and Nehemiah, thank you for supporting me and my endeavors. Thank you for loving me, especially when I do nothing without a pen and a clipboard, thank you for enduring my late nights, your ideas, the sounding board, the love and the support. Thank you for celebrating our legacy.

To my prayer partners and to my accountability partners, thank you for the long talks and the powerful prayers and the encouragement.

To the readers who this will reach and empower and touch and affect, may these words empower you and help you reach some resolve. May you be inspired to achieve your goals and dreams. May you enhance your relationship with God so that your other relationships will also improve. May you enhance your self-esteem through prayer and study. May you have courage and peace. Share love the best you can until you can share love without reservation.

A Working Marriage

Onedia N. Gage seeks to share her outlandish pursuit of life with her love and work ethic. She desires to share her advice with you in a manner that helps you do the same through her example. She hopes that these words will motivate you.

Please feel free to contact me and share your progress.
onediagage@onediagagespeaks.com, or @onediangage (twitter).
www.onediagagespeaks.com

Blogtalkradio.com/onediagage

Youtube.com/onediagage

Facebook.com/onediagage

A Working Marriage

On The Same Team

Coach ♦ Advocate ♦ Teacher ♦ Facilitator

Conference Speaker ♦ Workshop Leader

To invite Dr. Gage to speak at your school, business, or organization,

Please contact us at: www.onediagagespeaks.com

@onediangage (twitter) ♦ onediagage@onediagagespeaks.com ♦ facebook.com/onediagage

youtube.com/onediagage ♦ blogtalkradio.com/onediagage ♦ ongage (Instagram)

A Working Marriage

Publishing

Do you have a book you want to write, but do not know what to do?

Do you have a book you need to publish but do not know how to start?

Would publishing move your career forward?

Let us help

onediagage@purpleink.net ♦ www.purpleink.net

281.740.5143 ♦ 713.705.5530

www.ingramcontent.com/pod-product-compliance
Lightning Source LLC
Chambersburg PA
CBHW061802070526
44586CB00023B/2673